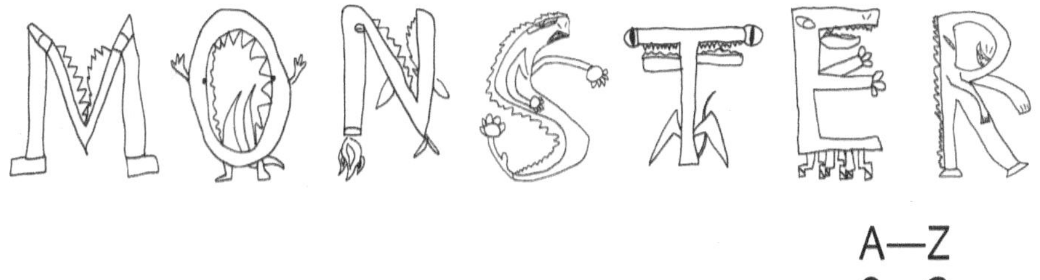

A—Z
0—9

Painter : Ryan Peden
Author : Josephine

Painter: Ryan Peden,10 years old, He sees everything in life as a monster. He is the expert of monster's painting and invention.

Author: Josephine, 12 years old, writing poetry and stories, painting.. She always feel that there is the other Josephine doing different things in another space.

The Monster Team

The Monster Team, an invisible organization, is created by a group of people who vow to fight against bad guys in the world.

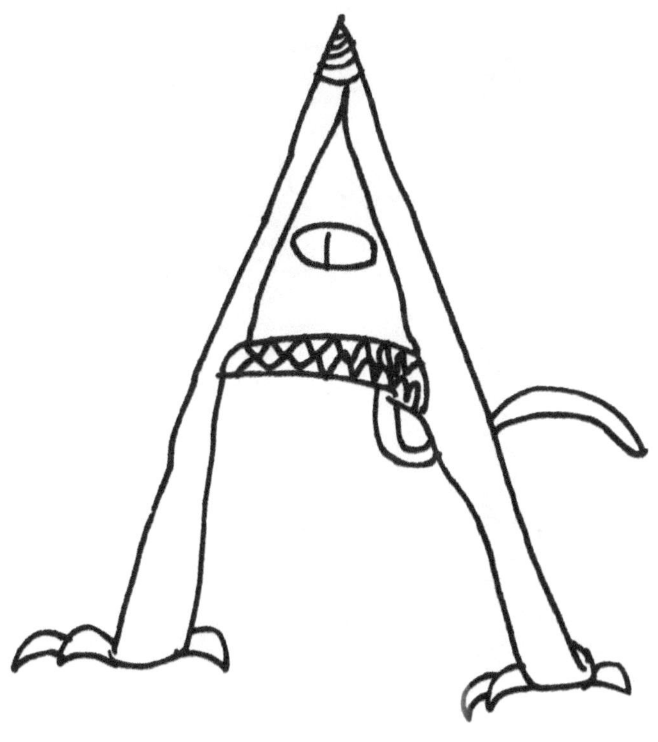

A stands for Alexander the Chief,
who likes to gossip.

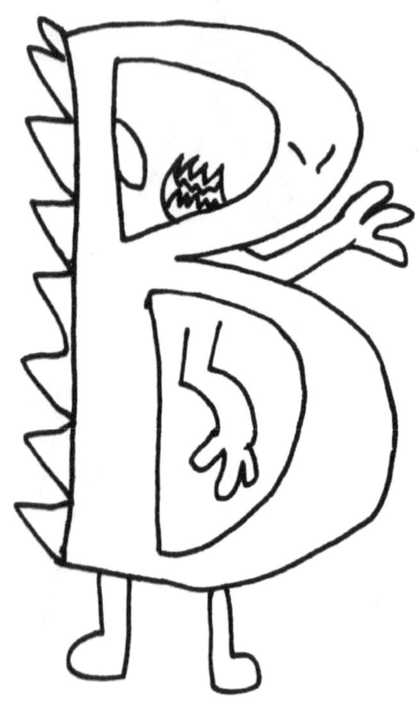

B stands for Brian the Spy,
who likes to keep secrets.

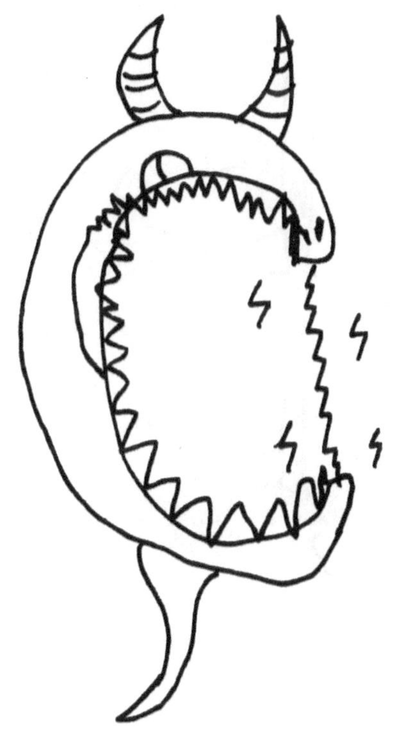

C stands for Cary the Lightning Cannon, who will shine.

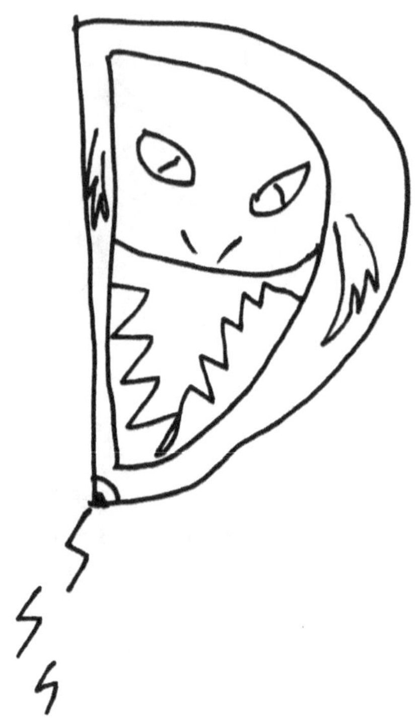

D stands for Derby the Intelligence,
who is good at writing reports.

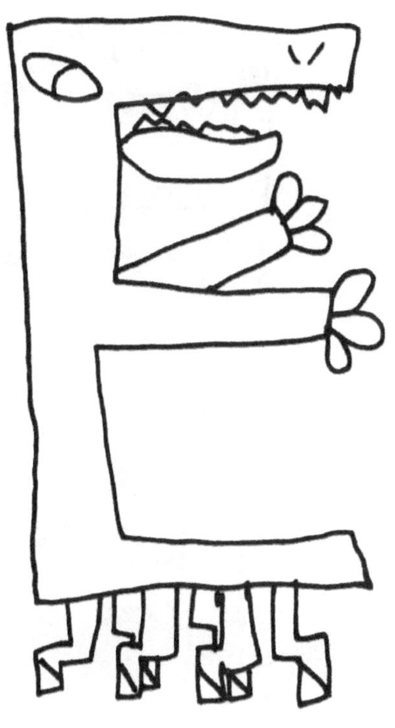

E stands for Ed the Cannon Fodder, who is a lazy guy.

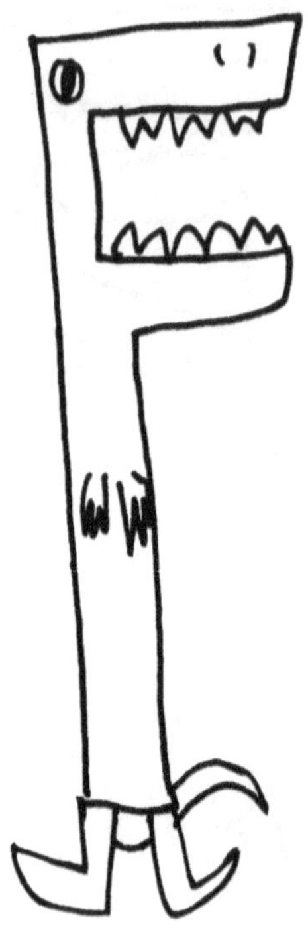

F stands for Frederick. He is my younger brother. He likes to eat.

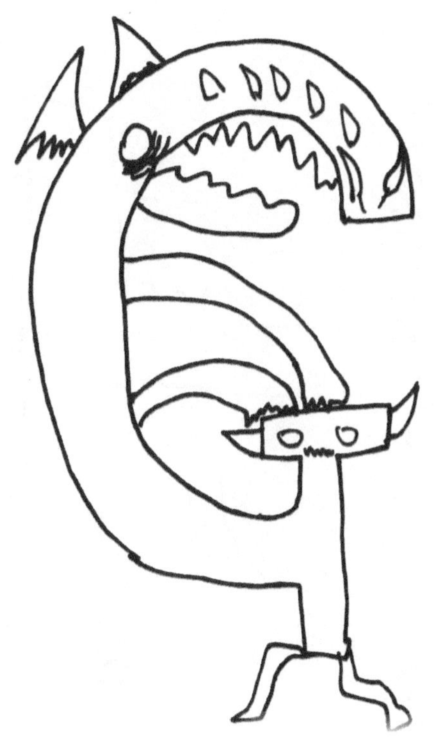

G stands for Guy. He is my neighbor. He likes to play piano.

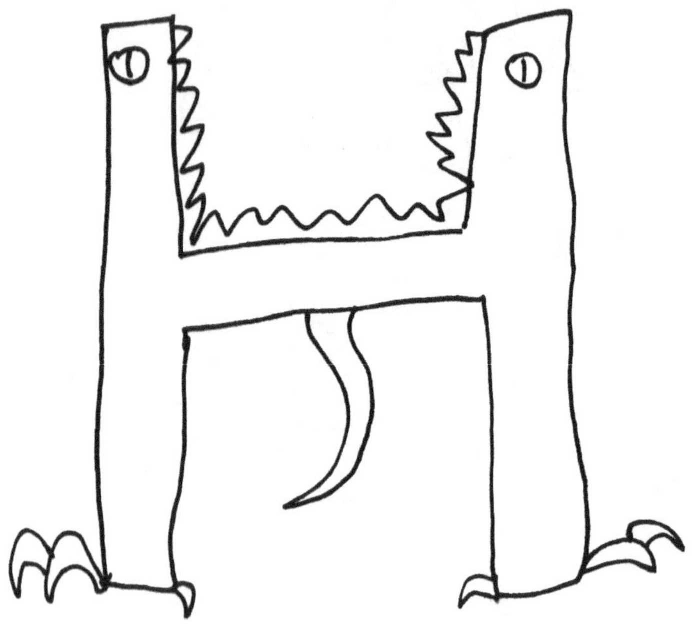

H stands for Homer the Wrestler,
who doesn't like running.

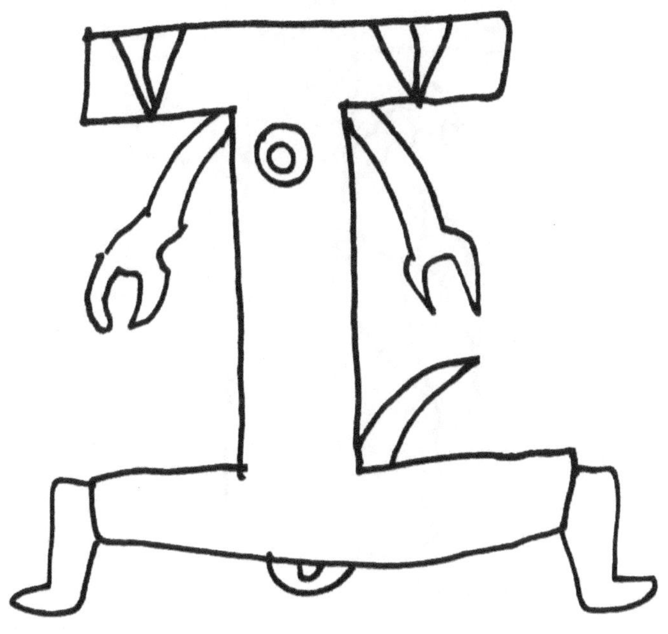

I stands for Ian. He is my eldest brother. He likes to fix things.

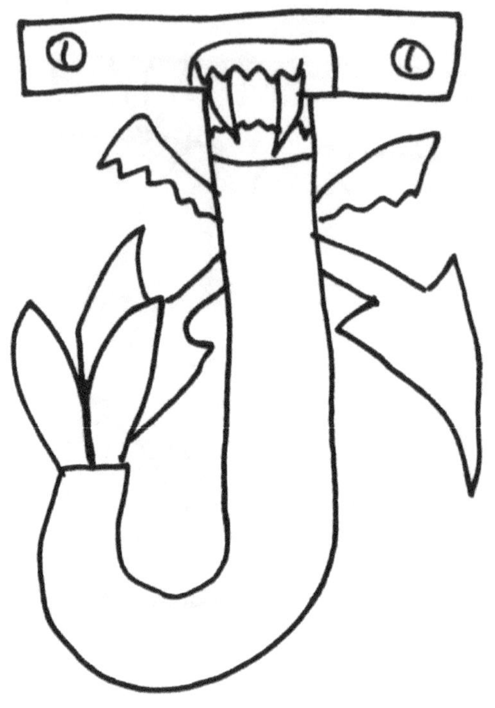

J stands for Jasper the Fighting Gold Claw, who likes flying.

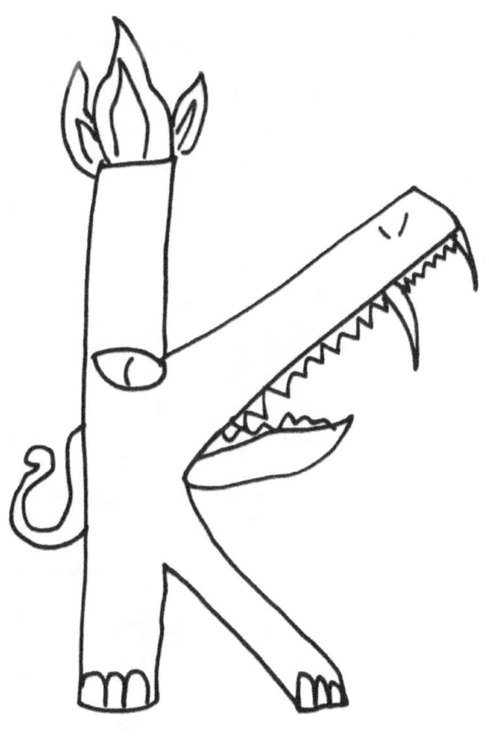

K stands for Kev the Lead Monkey,
who always orders others around.

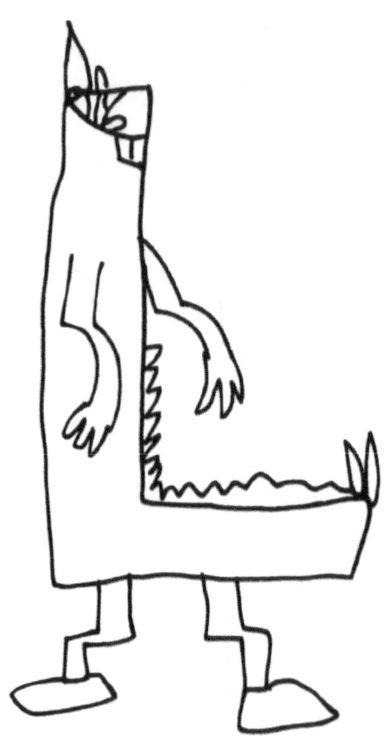

L stands for Larry the Mobile Monster Machine, who likes to shoot himself in the foot.

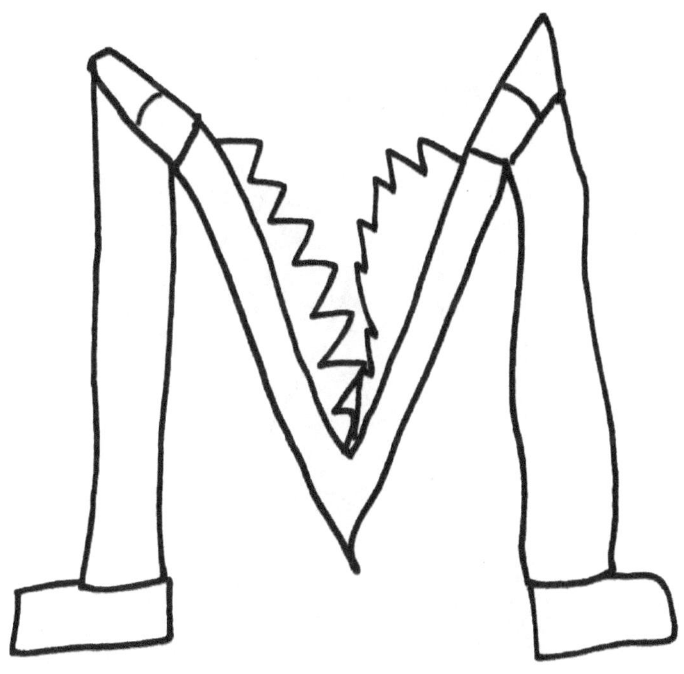

M stands for Mike. She is
my sister. She likes to eat at
McDonald's.

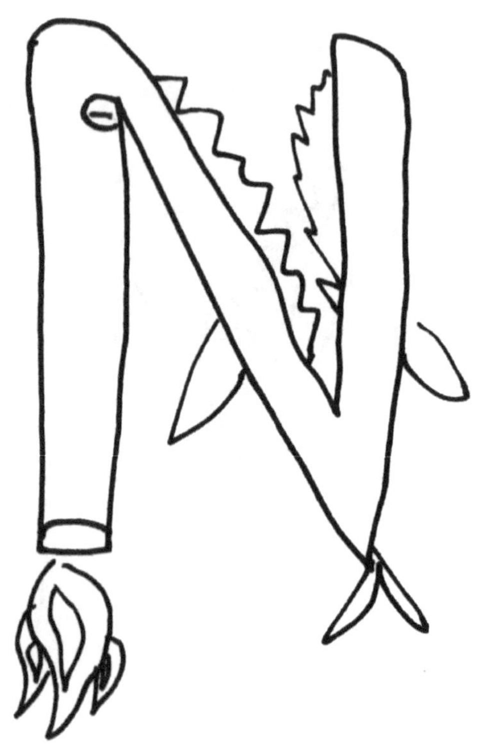

N stands for Neddy the Rage
God, who likes to barbecue.

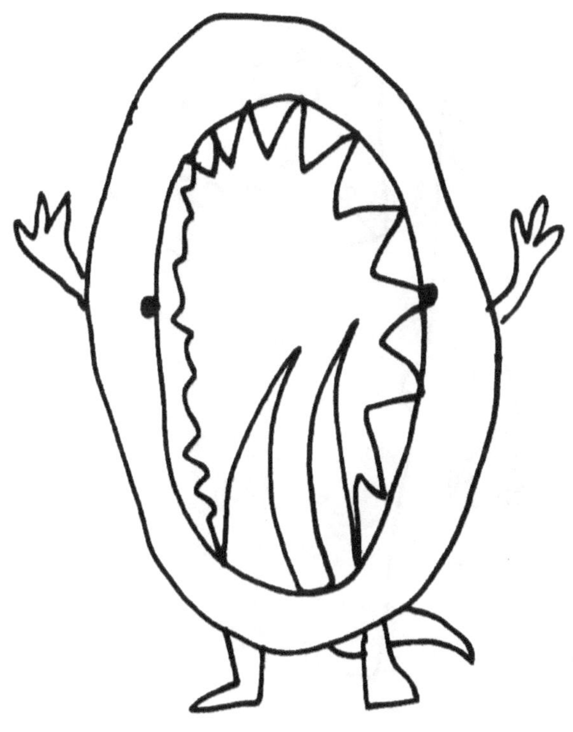

O stands for Oz the Typhoon Air Conditioner, who likes to cause troubles.

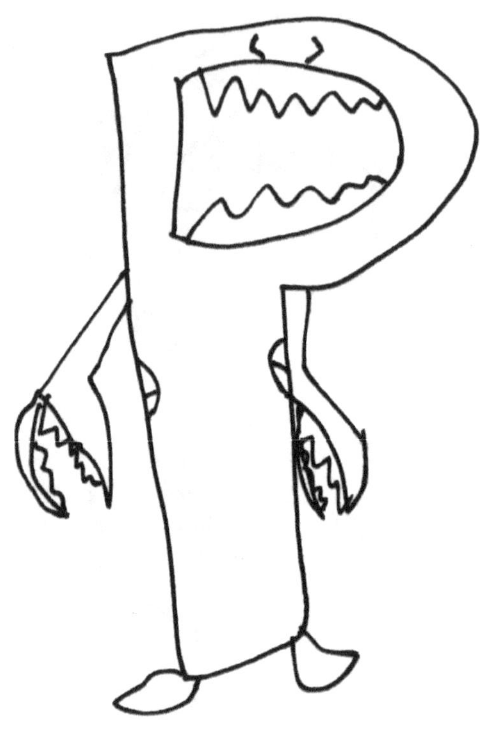

P stands for Philip the Scissors Freak, who likes gardening.

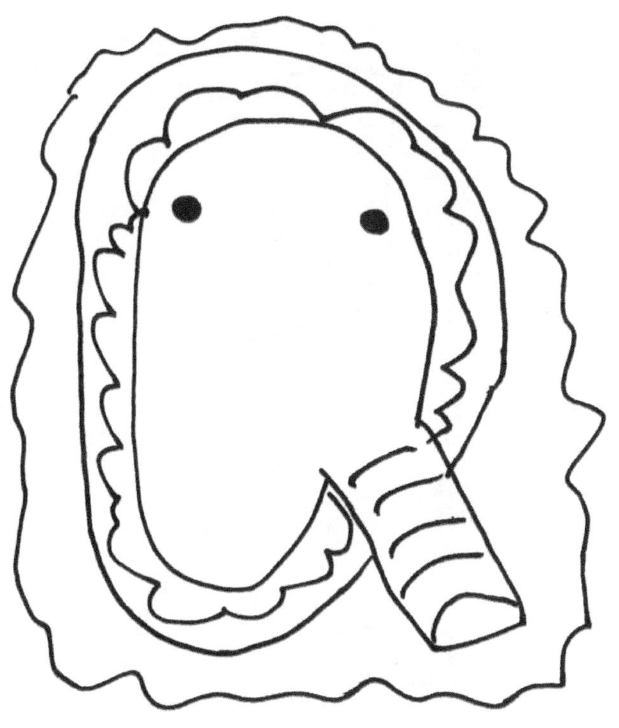

Q stands for Quentin.
He is my pet. He likes to sleep.

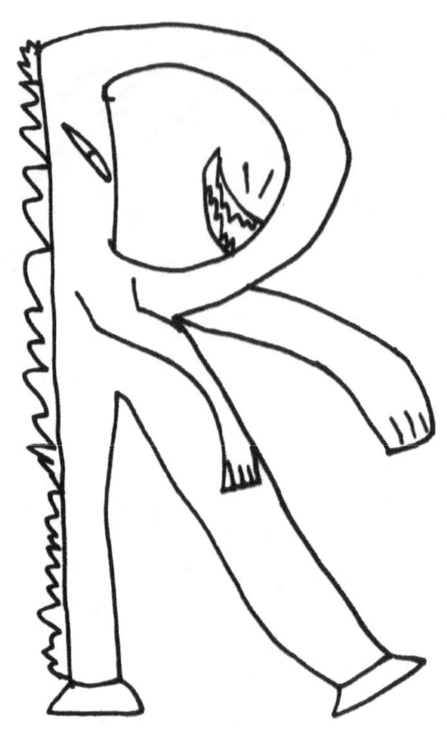

R stands for Rob.
He is my second eldest brother.
He giggles a lot.

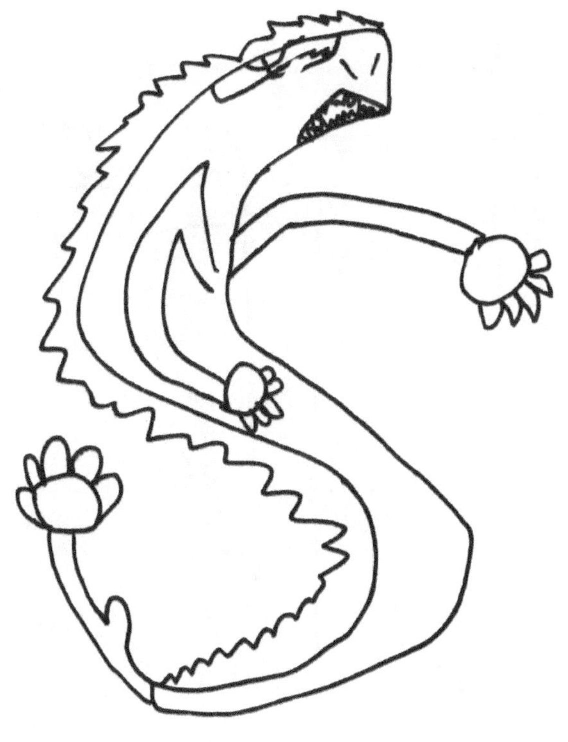

S stands for Seb the Mountaineer,
who likes to play with marmots.

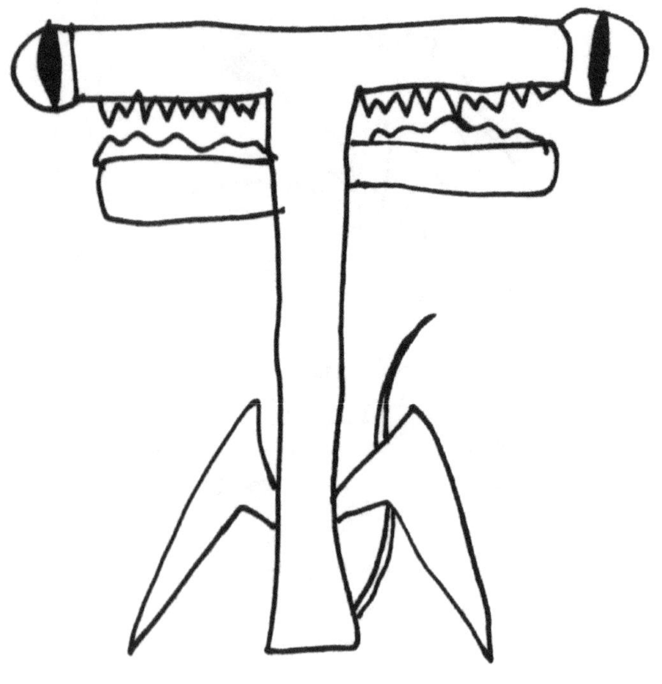

T stands for Tel. He is my uncle. He likes to shave.

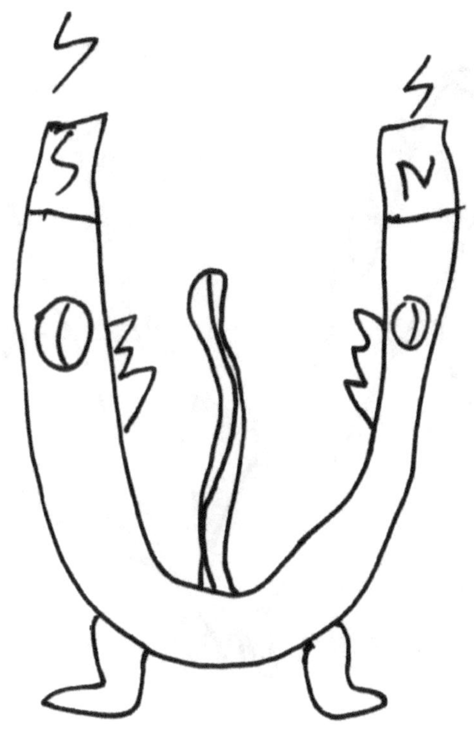

U stands for Urban the Bad Guy Sucker, who likes good guys.

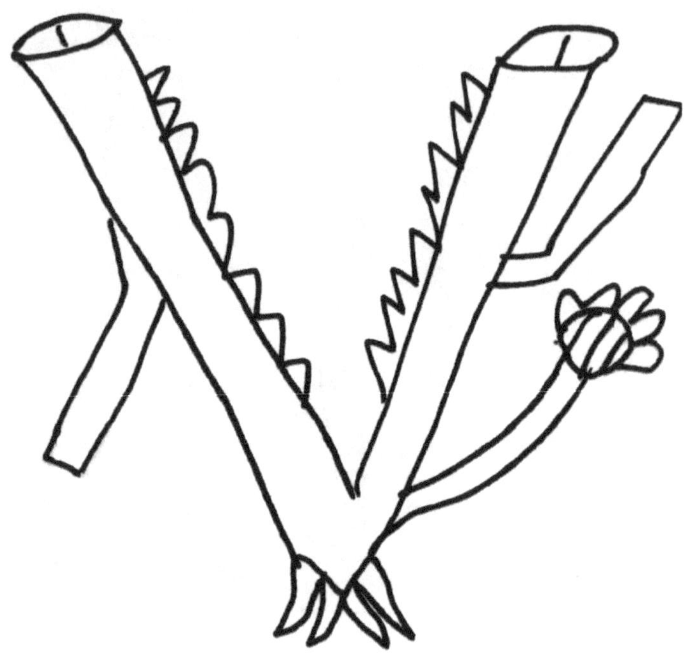

V stands for Vic the Liar Fairy,
who likes honest people.

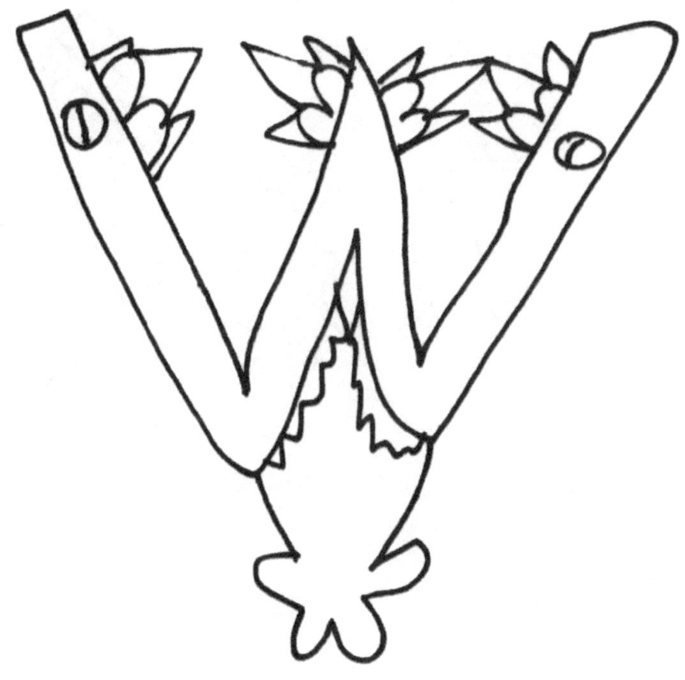

W stands for Well. She is my sister. She likes to fart.

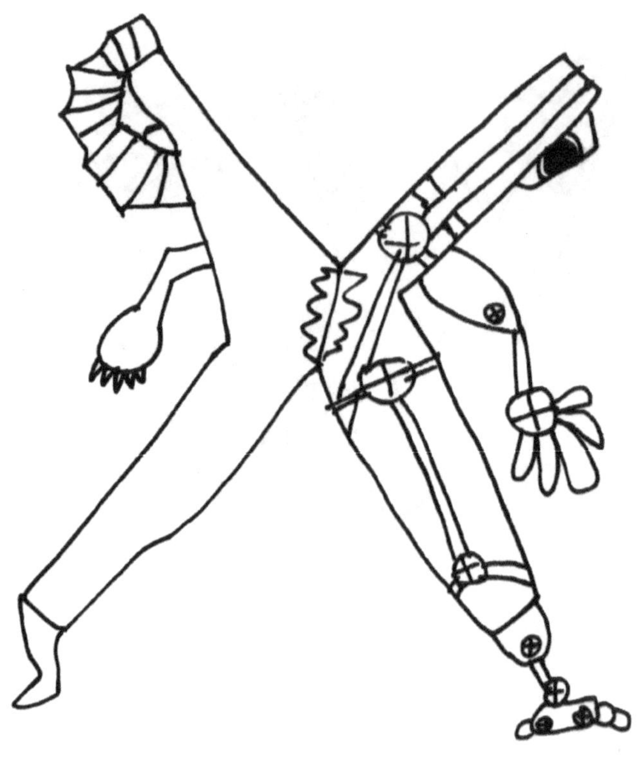

X stands for Xavier the Universal
Logistics Team, who is very nosy.

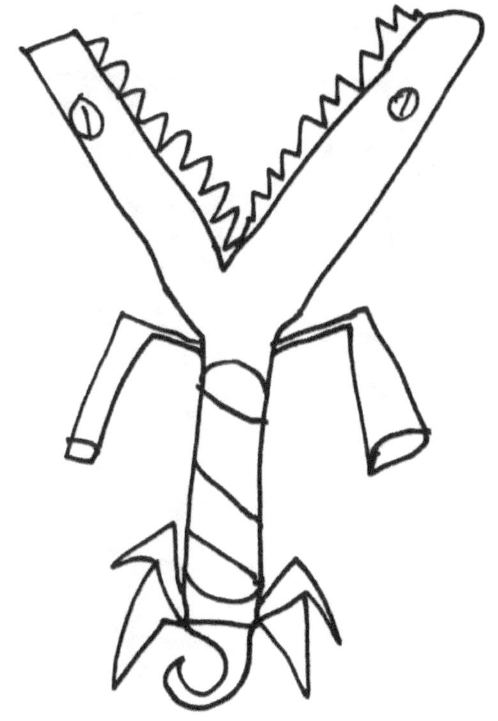

Y stands for Yuri. She is my sister. She likes screaming.

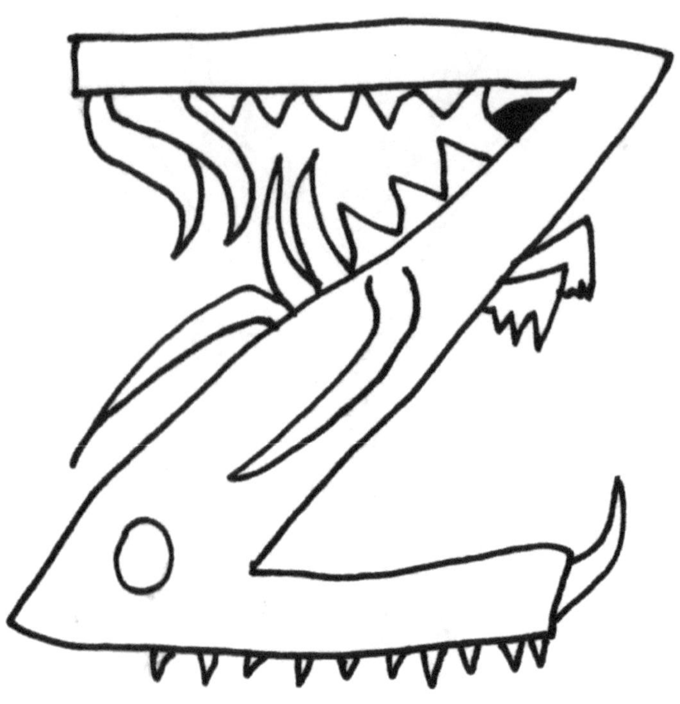

Z stands for Ziv thes Sea Monster, who likes to prank others.

The Sour Grapers

The Sour Grapers, also known as the Deformed Tissue, on the other hand, is created by another group of people, who like to do damage.

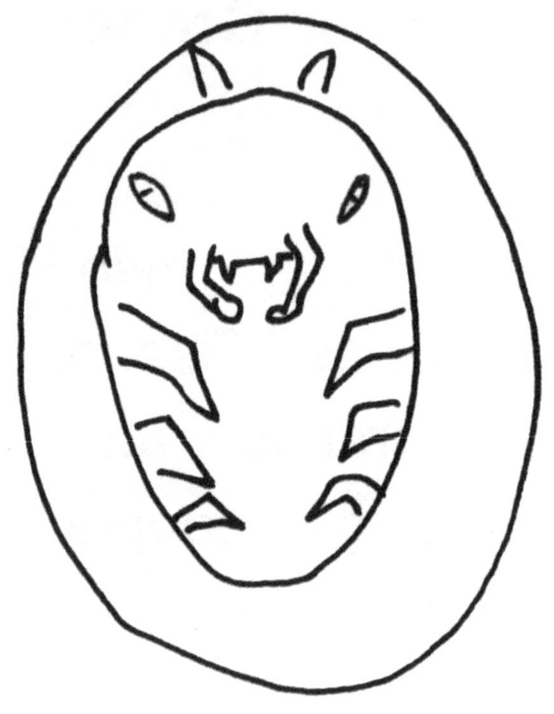

0 is a deformation beetle,
who hates downhill.

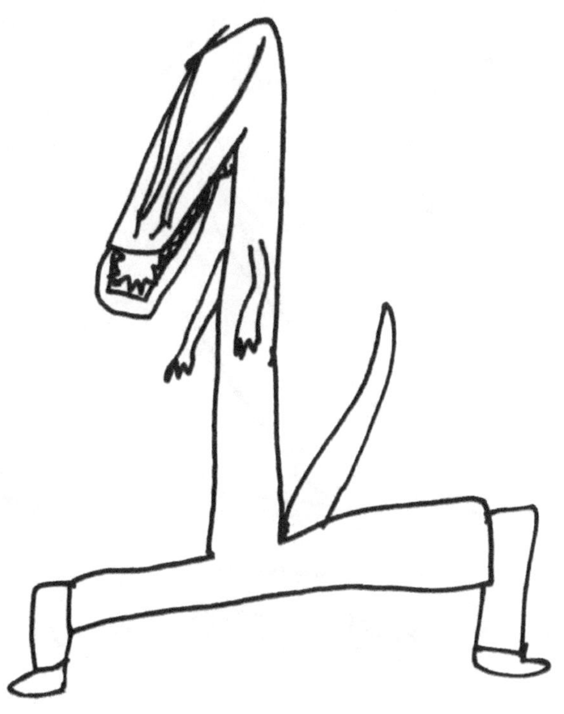

1 is a deformation mantis,
who hates standing .

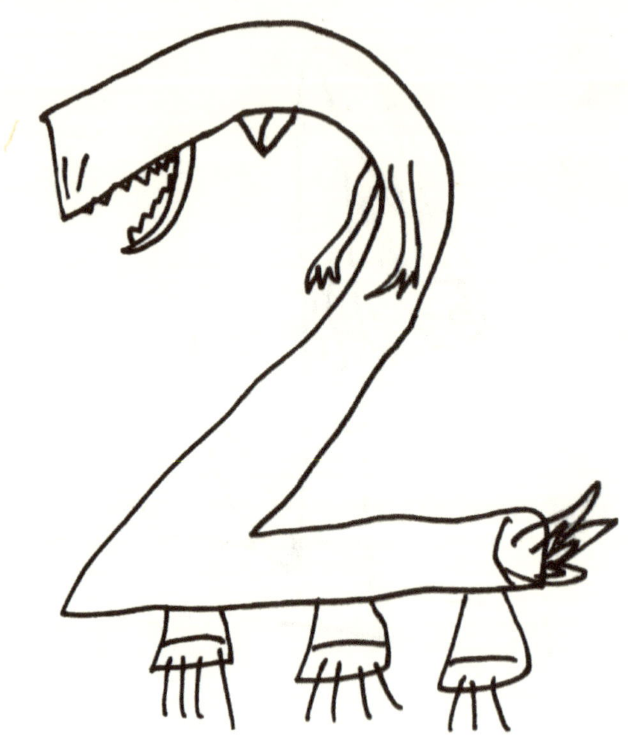

2 is a deformation centipede,
who is good at sneaking attack.

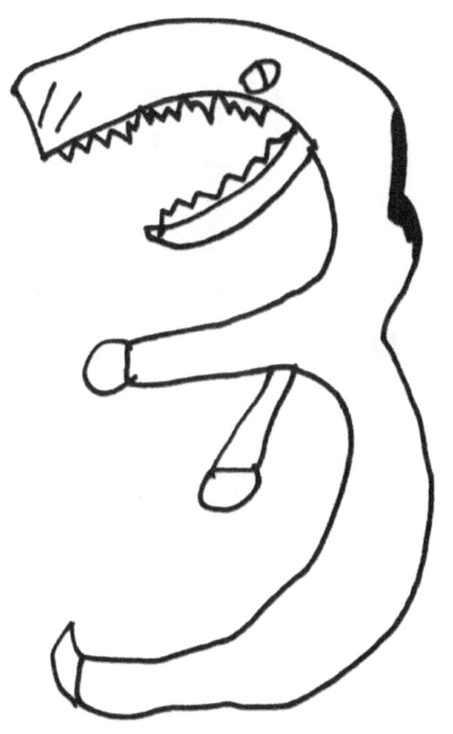

3 is a deformation Ant,
who is good at playing boxing.

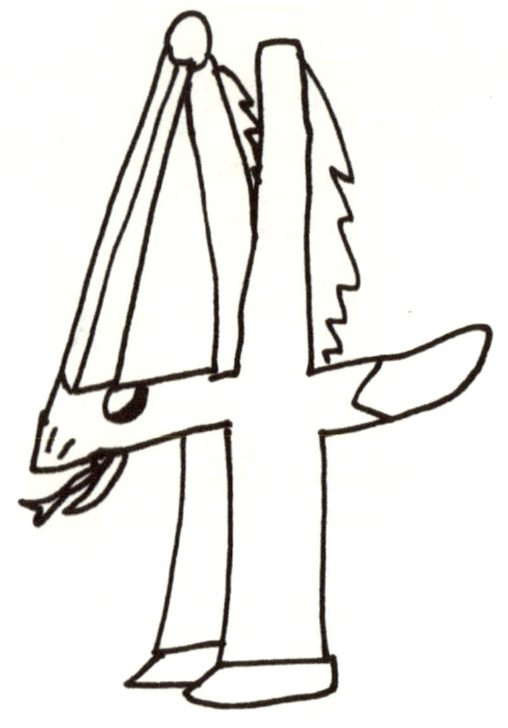

4 is a deformation moth,
who hates fighting.

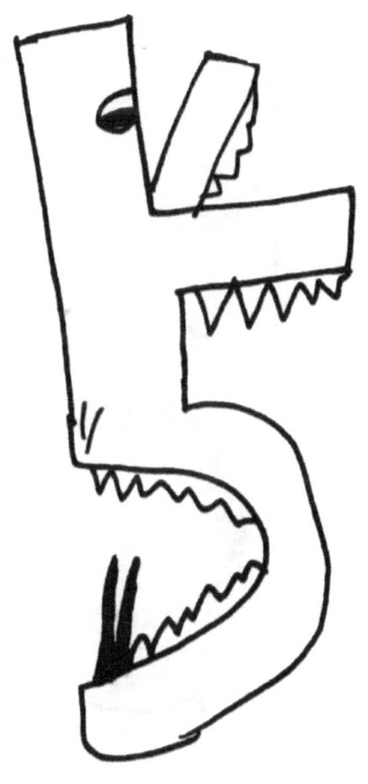

5 is a deformed snail,
who is good at biting people.

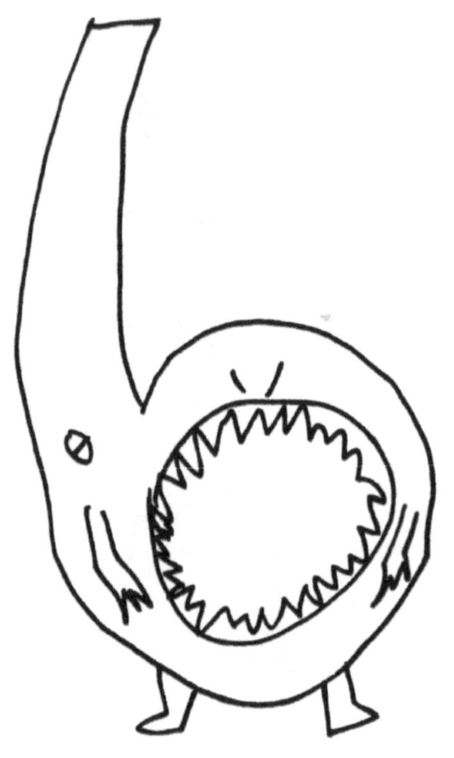

6 is a deformed ladybird,
who is good at trapping.

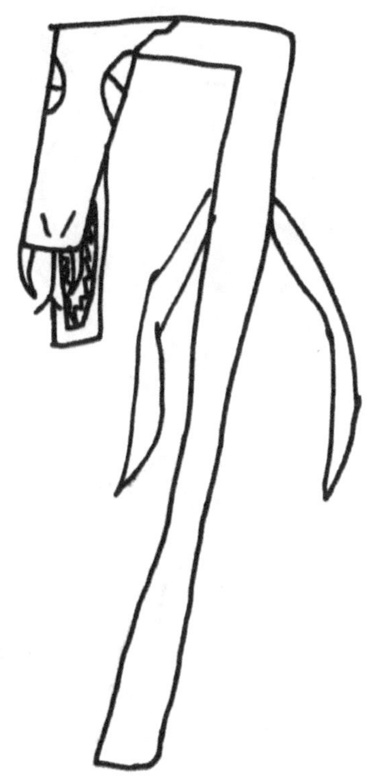

7 is a deformed damselfly,
who hates me very much.

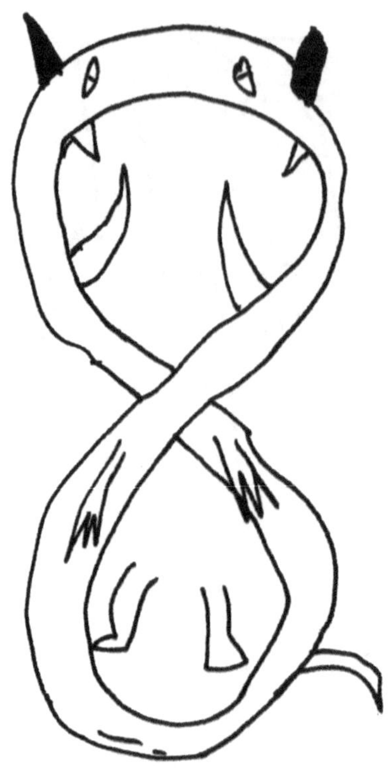

8 is a deformed caterpillar,
who is good at poisoning.

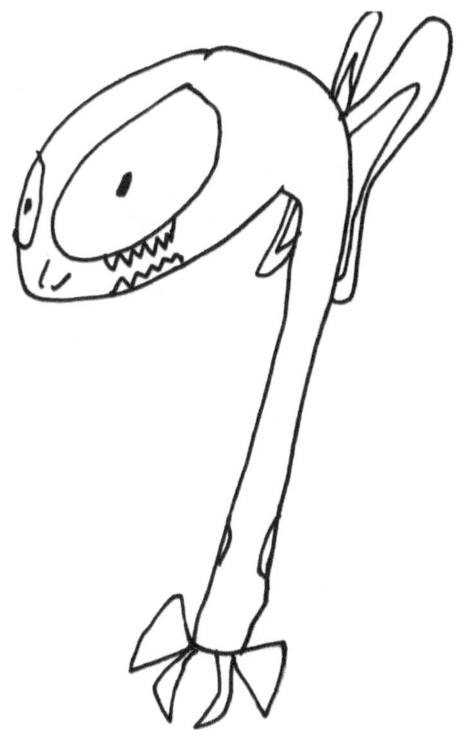

9 is a deformed bee,
who is good at arguing.

Monster

Author / Josephine

Painter / Ryan Peden

Editor / Matt Harsh , Sophia

Email: sophiapastry@gmail.com

Designer / Sandy

Email: sandyqmm@gmail.com

Publisher / EHGBooks United States

http://www.TaiwanFellowship.org

Date / February 2019

Distribution Channels

Online

Amazon.com

China

Xiamen International Book Company Limited

Add: 4 / F, Logistics Building, No.8, Yuehua Road,

Huli District, Xiamen City China

Direct Line / 0592-5061658、 6028707

Taiwan

Sanmin Bookstores / http://www.sanmin.com.tw

Add: No. 386, Fuxing N. Road, Taipei Taiwan

Add: No. 61, Chongqing S. Road, Taipei Taiwan

Direct Line / 02-2500-6600、 02-2361-7511

Kingstone Bookstores / http://www.kingstone.com.tw

Price / US$10 / NT$300 / RMB$68